VIDEO GAME REVOLUTION

PAID TO GAME

by Daniel Mauleón

raintree

a Capstone company — publishers for children

Raintree is an imprint of Capstone Global Library Limited, a company incorporated in England and Wales having its registered office at 264 Banbury Road, Oxford, OX2 7DY – Registered company number: 6695582

www.raintree.co.uk
myorders@raintree.co.uk

Editor: Gena Chester
Designers: Kay Fraser and Rachel Tesch
Media researcher: Tracy Cummins
Original illustrations © Capstone Global Library Limited 2020
Production Specialist: Kathy McColley
Originated by Capstone Global Library Ltd

ISBN 978 1 4747 8809 0 (hardback)
ISBN 978 1 4747 8815 1 (paperback)

British Library Cataloguing in Publication Data
A full catalogue record for this book is available from the British Library.

Acknowledgements
We would like to thank the following for permission to reproduce photographs: Alamy: Osterode Am Harz, 13; Getty Images: Eric_Ananmalay/ESPAT Media, 15; Newscom: Fabrizio Bensch/ REUTERS, 27; Shutterstock: Anna Chernova, Design Element, Anthony McLaughlin, 8, aurielaki, Cover 1, BlueSkyImage, 11, Casimiro PT, 7, Christos Georghiou, Design Element, Dean Drobot, 19, Designworkz, Design Element, FrameStockFootages, 29, Jirapong Manustrong, 22, Margot Petrowski, 5, PranThira, 20, ricochet64, 25, VasiliyBudarin, 17, VectorPixelStar, Design Element, yurakr, Design Element.

Every effort has been made to contact copyright holders of material reproduced in this book. Any omissions will be rectified in subsequent printings if notice is given to the publisher.

All the internet addresses (URLs) given in this book were valid at the time of going to press. However, due to the dynamic nature of the internet, some addresses may have changed, or sites may have changed or ceased to exist since publication. While the author and publisher regret any inconvenience this may cause readers, no responsibility for any such changes can be accepted by either the author or the publisher.

CONTENTS

RAKING IN COINS

Do you ever wish you could be Mario, making sure you grab every last coin? Many video-game fans want the same thing. More people are playing video games than ever before. When they're not playing, they are looking for other things to enjoy about games.

FACT!

In 2017, 666 million people watched gaming videos.

More and more people are creating content for gaming fans around the world. These people are called Content Creators. They use tools to make all kinds of videos, from **playthroughs** to game reviews. **Streamers** share long play sessions with fans live. **Developers** make everything from visual effects to the code that makes video games run. Just like Mario, all these people want to collect coins for their work – but real ones!

developer a person who creates computer software
playthrough the act of playing a video game from start to finish
streamer a person who shares footage online of video-game play

LIGHTS, CAMERA AND VIDEO-GAME ACTION

2

A popular way to make money from video games is by recording game play and sharing it creatively. Streamers **broadcast** their games online and let the world watch as they play. Content creators edit and create video-game footage to share online. Starting either a streaming or a content-creating channel can be a challenge. These gamers need expensive equipment to play games, record and more.

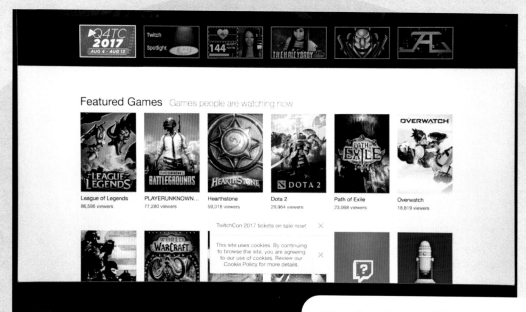

To start streaming, a gamer needs to create an account on a streaming website. Twitch, YouTube, Periscope and Mixer are all streaming sites. Depending on what games the streamer wants to play, there are different steps to starting a stream.

broadcast to send out a programme on TV, internet or radio

moderate to monitor a chat room and delete inappropriate content

Twitch talk

The biggest video-game streaming website is Twitch. Twitch connects more than 2 million streamers to 15 million daily viewers. With so many options, it's easy to find a game and streamer you want to watch. A big part of Twitch streams is the chat. Viewers can send public messages to the streamer. They can also send messages to others watching. It is important for streamers to keep an eye on bullying in the chat. Some streamers use bots to watch for bad language. Others have fans who **moderate** the chat. If viewers break the rules, moderators and bots can remove their messages from the channel.

CONSOLES

Newer consoles like the PlayStation 4 and Xbox One have built-in streaming abilities. However, players are limited on these systems. They cannot customize their stream or stream older games. If players want to stream older games, capture more content and have better quality in their stream, they use a capture card. A capture card is a piece of technology that looks like a small box. It connects to a player's console, TV and computer. The card splits the image and sound of the game. Then it sends the signal to both the TV and the computer.

The Xbox One console and controller

COMPUTERS

Players can also play and stream games directly on their computers. When streaming from a computer, players need special **software** programs. Many streaming programs have extra features. Players can customize their stream with images to add their own style. They can also install tools to add sound effects, play music, track their gaming stats and display their stream chat.

Once they load a game, the software shares their screen online for others to watch. It can take a powerful computer to run both games and streaming software. Sometimes streamers use two computers. One runs the game, and another runs the stream using a capture card.

FACT!

After a game has been captured on a card, some streamers edit their video afterwards with effects, filters and transitions.

software a program used by a computer

THE COST OF STREAMING

The price for a gaming computer can range from £400 ($500) to £3,300 ($4,000). For streamers playing older games or games with simple graphics, a £400 computer can get the job done. If a streamer wants to play newer games at higher settings, they will need to spend more. For console streamers, a new Xbox One or PS4 can cost between £100 ($120) and £300 ($360). Serious streamers may need to buy additional equipment. Common tools streamers use are cameras, microphones and lights.

It is not cheap to begin streaming. For professional streamers, it's worthwhile for them to have a powerful computer. This gives them more options of what to stream. With more games to stream, they have a chance to make more money.

LEVEL UP! BUILDING A BRAND AND MAKING MONEY

$ ▤

3

The biggest streamers work hard to stand out from the competition. They create unique **brands** and usernames for their online profiles. Usernames keep real identities safe and help complete brand identities.

brand a name that identifies a product or manufacturer, such as Apple, Sony or Microsoft

Streamers build brands in a few different ways. Some streamers only play certain kinds of games. Their channel may focus on puzzle games like *Tetris* and *Portal*. They might stream only one game, such as *Minecraft*, to appeal to that game's specific fan base. Other streamers build a personality. Maybe a streamer is very funny and makes a lot of jokes while streaming.

Talented streamers draw attention to how well they play games. Speedrunners stream themselves beating a game as quickly as possible. They compete for world records or just to beat their own. YellowKillerBee is a speedrunner who plays a lot of platforming games, such as *Super Mario Sunshine* or *Celeste*.

ABOUT THE MONEY $

Streamers who are serious about making cash work hard to gain a lot of followers. They do this by building a brand and streaming regularly. It can take a long time. Ninja, a streamer, has the largest following on Twitch. He did not become popular overnight. He has been playing competitively for more than 10 years and streaming professionally for more than 5 years. Once he started playing *Fortnite*, he went from 500,000 viewers to 12 million. It is important for streamers to like what they do. Once they have big followings, there are three main ways to make money: tips, **subscribers** and **sponsorships**.

sponsorship financial support, usually in return for public acknowledgement
subscriber a person who pays money to watch a streaming channel

The streamer Ninja

FACT!
Streaming websites allow audiences to give small amounts of money as tips to streamers. With a big enough following, tips can add up.

SUBSCRIBERS AND SPONSORS

Twitch lets fans subscribe to their favourite channels. Fans pay each month to get extra features on the channel. These subscribed fans get **advertisement**-free streams, can use special emojis and view subscriber-only videos. The money from subscriptions is split between the streamer and Twitch.

Streamers can also make money through sponsorships with companies. For example, a company that makes headsets may send money and a headset to a streamer. The streamer uses the headset and shares what they like about it. The streamer receives free equipment and cash, and the headset company gets noticed by viewers of the stream. Some of these fans may buy the headset for themselves. Sponsorships can be for streaming gear, clothes, snacks, gaming chairs and other products.

advertisement a notice that calls attention to a product or an event

FACT!
In 2017 viewers gave tips to Twitch streamers 22.55 million times!

CREATING CONTENT

4

Not all players want to stream. Creators make videos and share them online. The more popular the video, the more money these creators earn. Many use the same equipment as streamers, such as cameras and microphones.

They also use programs for recording and editing videos. These programs let them mix and cut the video-game footage they've recorded. Content creators make all kinds of videos. Easy Allies is a successful group of creators on YouTube. They have over 200,000 subscribers.

LET'S PLAYS

Let's Plays are videos that feature creators playing through games. However, these aren't live and may be edited to be shorter. Creators add commentary with jokes, tips or their own reactions. You may see groups of players create Let's Plays and have a conversation during game play.

FAN FILMS

Some creative players use special software to create short, animated fan films. Video software lets them use characters, maps, sounds and more from games to tell their own stories. It's like taking action figures from your favourite TV shows and creating new stories about them.

FACT!
In a 2016 survey, one in three gamers said they watch Let's Play streams and videos regularly.

VIDEO-GAME REVIEWS

Some gamers have a lot of opinions. One way they like to share them is by creating review videos. They play through games and capture footage. While playing, they take notes about what they like and don't like about a game. After playing, gamers write a review and record themselves reading it. Finally, they edit the video. They combine clips of the game with the audio of their review.

OTHER CONTENT

There are endless options available. Some content creators make videos about the history of video games or about making video games. Others have news channels where they share gaming updates and their reactions.

MAKING MONEY ON YOUTUBE

   Most creators upload their videos to YouTube. Like streamers, it is important for YouTubers to build a brand. They might focus on reviews or have a few kinds of videos. Either way, they want new followers to watch their videos. YouTubers can set up their videos to earn money from advertisements. Each time someone watches an ad at the beginning of a video, the creator makes fractions of a pound. The exact number varies, but YouTubers report earning about £2–£8 for every 1,000 views. For many that's not enough to live off, but it could help support a gaming hobby. Some people make a great deal of money. DanTDM, a YouTuber who creates *Minecraft* content, earned £13.75 million ($16.5 million) in 2017.

PROFESSIONAL JOBS 5

Many people also get paid to make video games. These creators are called developers. Developers may work on independent games in small teams or for larger companies. They may program the games, make art or music for games, or write the stories. Developers all must work together to create a great game.

FACT!

Electronic Arts (EA) is one of the largest gaming companies and has over 9,000 employees. They make everything from sports games to action games to role-playing games.

Job	Duty	Salary
Director	Manages all the teams involved. They help guide everyone to create a finished game.	£30,000-£110,000
Designer	Builds the game. How should it play? What are the levels like? They work with the other teams to make this a reality.	£30,000-£90,000
Programmer	Creates all the code running in the background of the game. They turn controller inputs into on-screen changes. They also test the game and fix computer errors.	£30,000-£75,000
Visual artist	Creates art early on to guide the creation of the game. They can make 2D or 3D models of characters or locations in the game. Animators, a type of visual artist, even make models move.	£25,000-£60,000
Sound design	Creates sound effects from recordings or with computers. Composers craft music to play in the background of games.	£25,000-£75,000
Writer	Creates character dialogue and in-game instructions. In games with big story lines, they also write and plan the plot.	£25,000-£65,000

Professional players

Just like athletic games, video games also have professional players. E-sports professionals play video games competitively to win money. They compete in tournaments alone or on teams. Some video games including *Overwatch* and *NBA 2k* even have official leagues. If you're not skilled enough to be an e-sports athlete, you can work in the industry. E-sports needs coaches, managers – even production crews for tournaments.

The PUBG Global Invitational 2018, an e-sports tournament

PRESS START

Are you interested in being paid to game? Time to get some practice! Next time you have friends over, take turns playing and talking. Take time to think about what your channel would be about. Want to create game reviews? Keep a journal as you play and take notes. What would you call it? Who would be your audience? Or maybe you want to create games? What kind of developer would you like to be? Before you know it, you may have a chance to make your dream gaming job a reality.

FACT!
Gamers interested in making games should visit Code.org. The site has projects that teach users how to code. It even has *Minecraft* tutorials.

Glossary

advertisement a notice that calls attention to a product or an event

brand a name that identifies a product or manufacturer, such as Apple, Sony or Microsoft

broadcast to send out a programme on TV, internet or radio

developer a person who creates computer software

moderate to monitor a chat room and delete inappropriate content

playthrough the act of playing a video game from start to finish

software a program used by a computer

sponsorship financial support, usually in return for public acknowledgement

streamer a person who shares footage online of video-game play

subscriber a person who pays money to watch a streaming channel

Find out more

Computer Games Designer (The Coolest Jobs on the Planet),
Mark Featherstone (Raintree, 2014)

E-sports Revolution (Video Game Revolution), Daniel Mauleón
(Raintree, 2020)

STEAM Jobs for Gamers (STEAM Jobs), Sam Rhodes (Raintree, 2018)

*Video Game Trivia: What You Never Knew about Popular Games,
Design Secrets and the Coolest Characters* (Not Your Ordinary Trivia),
Sean McCollum (Raintree, 2018)

Websites

Common Sense Media: game reviews
www.commonsensemedia.org/game-reviews

Gamefroot: game editor
make.gamefroot.com/

Minecraft Hour of Code tutorials
code.org/minecraft

Index